D1460149

Gallery Books
Editor Peter Fallon

THE VIEW FROM HERE

Sara Berkeley

THE VIEW FROM HERE

Gallery Books

The View from Here
is first published
simultaneously in paperback
and in a clothbound edition
on 14 October 2010.

The Gallery Press
Loughcrew
Oldcastle
County Meath
Ireland

www.gallerypress.com

ISBN 978 1 85235 497 8 *paperback*
       978 1 85235 498 5 *clothbound*

A CIP catalogue record for this book
is available from the British Library.

Contents

for Talc

Minor Star

I was born on a raw March afternoon,
a Tuesday, the rain a benediction. Nevertheless

my mother could not bring me home.
O thirsty water, O hungry food.

All that week the sun tried to break through.
I was not eating. I was waiting.

Just a whisper of myself. All the clutter,
the complications, stayed on the ground.

I was further up, breathing,
not sad or happy yet, not even watching,

just looking, my round brown week-old eyes
ablaze like the sun, our ball of fire,

our minor star. Eventually the doctors solved the puzzle.
My mother took me home to the waiting brothers

and I began to climb the staircase of my life,
every day living a little, dying a little;

this milestone, that milestone. Prometheus
walked out of Olympus with his fennel stalk

of fire, took away from us
all knowledge of the future;

put all evil in a jar, war and quarrel,
hatred and desire.

I've been carrying it, strapped
to my head, this far. I do not want

to open it. Some days I shake with the fear
of life, some days with joy.

The Habit of Laughter

I have been in the habit of living
with poetry and wild laughter
and a glass of wine in the evening.

The sky has repeatedly fallen
and been nailed up again.
Dictators have wrought havoc

but my habit of laughing
in the face of despair
will not be broken — not with love

being airlifted from the scene
in a body bag; not with
repeated loss of the best;

not even with my life resembling
a buckled guitar in the back
of a hopelessly jaded car.

There never has been a cure
for all the bell tolling,
the frets inciting the strings

to longing, the drift of blossoms
down the curve of a summer evening,
nor the wail of the last train leaving.

Again and again we experience
brief moments of rapture
only we can understand.

Some things are better left
unplanned. But laughter?
Now there's a reason

to march down Main Street
in your boots with your trumpet
and your heart in a suitcase.

Carrying

Spring comes into our valley along the deer paths
unpinning birdsong as she walks;
she is the best dressed and the kindest;
we all want to invite her to our homes
and have her stay among us.

I cannot resist
stealing along her nights with their lovely dark,
songs to the moon and the youngest stars,
the wash of the dawn on every leaf,
the grace.

It was a spring like this,
I was with my daughter on the mountain;
I let her go where she would
among the wild iris and the blue-eyed grass;
she filled her basket, she was overflowing.

Those were the days
when her thoughts were still written on her face,
when I began at last to understand
my own mother's sleepless nights
and the fury of her love.

And though the past
is a dress I'll always wear
I am putting on a new one,
letting the old threads fall to the grass,
free as the hills.

On the trail home
I drink from a stream
as though thirst had just been invented.
Beneath the crowding of the leaves
and the cries of birds

the stillness holds,
and into the stillness
comes my knowing:
we carry our daughters until they are too light to bear,
then we carry our mothers; they are heavy as air.

Night Horses

What I remember of it was the melancholy
innocence of those first rings on the river

and later the darker smudged fingers of rain
weaving the standing water into a garment with no seam.

The flood began to fill some ancient hollow,
then overflowed that pool, found a new level

and began to rise: rain at the back of my throat,
behind my eyes, the silk of it in my mouth.

It ran through all the corridors of my house,
found the many corners, carried the pieces of my past,

a tide of fragments at the high-water mark;
it tugged at me as it went by, a lunar pull,

and, as the chambers filled, the weight of rain
began to turn my world so slowly upside down

the sky emptied its pockets; into the river
fell the milky moon and its veil of stars,

and into the running stream I dropped my natural joy.
Down it went, catching the light, a silver depth charge,

until it met the river bed. On the surface
I stopped pitching, found my stillness,

and up from the submerged world
with its upside-down roofs and chimneys

rode the night horses with their unbridled stories,
and after them the green dawn and the songs of drowning.

A Poem About Happiness

It would begin like this:
a man in his overcoat, head bowed,
walking from end to end of his town
in the armour of his life, not so much heavy
as close-fitting, a kind of light chain mail
he pulls on at the break of every day.
Some nights he never takes it off.
Those are the nights he dreams.

It would go on, through innocence of mornings
in his pale green rooms,
the ease of days, philosophy and song
the unlikely companions of this man
who turns his collar up against the world, at whom
the world stares back without a sign.

Consider this:
the dew that collects by itself
on the grass that finds a crack in the slab
is enough to slake his thirst,
and that is why he thrives on so little love

and why it finishes thus:
with evening lush around his house,
the spring trees almost all dressed, the oaks,
black locusts, only the silks holding out;
and a moment on a cluttered street —
happiness from nowhere;
it rises like the first glorious journey
of a childhood kite, like distant voices
from one of those unplanned
all summer evening long
football games that nobody wants to end,
that go on and on and on
until the light fails.

Dark Summer Days

I have written my daughter to sleep.
She lies in the other bed among her books and toys,
the bowed and weathered instruments of her navigation.

In fragile possession of her course
and her own short set of ship's orders
she steps bravely out with me onto the burning waters.

We travel in this single room
where the nails are growing out of the wood
and the paint flakes off the window ledge.

On dark summer days when rising is difficult
this is my Parisian garret, my narrow turret,
my writer's attic with its high beams and precious dust;

it is here I hunker down and shout into the dark,
some nights nothing, some nights
starbursts of language, jubilant at their release.

Across the fearless moon
hastens what little sky we can see; what few trees
stand in the mornings with their arms out;

through every time zone their same song
fills the loudness of our being alone,
together, in the gentle rocking of our sea-glass room.

In her sleep my girl is made of sand,
but at first light she's a young redwood
driving up like a mast through the sea foam;

and as for me, even if no words come,
I'll be here waiting by the window in the pre-dawn
before the birds.

Swimming Pool

I have fallen for water,
a silky bolt of it, rolling and unrolling
under the heavy sky.

This was where
I saw the first girl swimming;
when she came up from a dive
I was kneeling by the water,
a makeshift altar.
I did not call out to her.

And this is where
I swim each evening around six;
sun slanting through the olive tree
breaks life down to its simplest concerns.

If I did not have her
there would be no more summer
and the darkness would not go
with the night.

The Business of Rain

This Saturday morning
we are not washing clothes
or cleaning house —
we are going about
the business of rain.

Late October, sometimes early,
five months of heat and dust
surrender their devils, give up their ghosts;
the world comes alive in russet and silvery green,
the world is washed clean.

She opens the windows,
she opens all the doors;
she is the small daughter
of the goddess of women and girls,
of water and the sea,

and she bursts upon the great outdoors
in her flip-flops and her summer cotton;
she takes joy and brings it to a new high;
she places it like a star in the treetops
and flies back to my side.

Angels fly like that,
butterflies and winged things,
fairies number her among their own,
she says, and I believe her.
I believe her. Yes, I do.

Heart's Desire

As soon as I left our house,
the girls in the back of the car
with their dolls and boards
and the promise of ice-cream,
the gates of happiness
opened wide as a mile
and we drove through laughing,
bringing our own weather.

When we got to the shore the ocean was there
in all its moods and moons, knocking against
the poles of the tides, lapping over our boards,
warm and choppy in the early afternoon.
Come in, she said, I'll show you how
to lie with your head in my tent.
No more bruises, I will lick your wounds,
for I am your element.

She rocked me back and forth
with the small swell of occasional boats
and I sank my head into her muffled reedy world.
How we rise above
fear and the fear of fear! Looking back,
the shore as metaphor, I saw
the small girls on their postage-stamp towels
shaking out diamonds with their starfish hands.

Approaching Eight

for Jessie

At first light
you get in your little boat,
it's tippy, and there's no one on the shore,
nobody waving.

In a photo of a million faces
I could find your face.
My finger would be drawn to it
even if I didn't look.

I never thought
eight would be so fragile,
so delicate, so robust, such a synthesis,
a symphony, a gallery full
of astonishing art. For my part,
now and then,
I see where I held the brush.

So off you go in your wooden boat
with the warped oars and peeling paint.
I won't stand guard on the shore.
I won't even peek
from the top window of the house
as you punt inexpertly round the lagoon.

I will close the door of an inner room;
and when you come home
with a crab's leg you found for me,
still dripping, faintly clicking,
we'll have cinnamon toast
and tea.

You'll clamber on my knee,
all elbows and long toes.
I might murmur,
Have fun on the water?
and you'll nod, not mentioning
how grown up it felt, how scary,
that moment when the oar
rode up, what a relief
to make it back to shore,
how tomorrow you want more.

And for a while,
in the quiet ticking
of our allotted time,
we won't do anything
together, but you will sit
enchanted vigil with your life
and I with mine.

Sacrificed

Today is a house, tiled walls, paint on paint,
late sun blowing, some bird insisting
it is eight o'clock.

The scrub jays sound like crickets in the heat.
They are coming down the street, my son,
my other daughter; she is riding on his back
with her arms around his neck;
they are going where they go with folded wings.

Above this house the sky is showing
that late summer evening white shine.
My love for them is alone, prowling
the back alleys, fierce-eyed, animal soft —
it finds them in the mornings
laid out in the white tent of their sleep,
sacrificed.

Before he was born I dreamed this boy —
he was choosing me and I chose him —
and later, when the girls were ready,
one by one, it was their turn
to let me in.

But when they think of childhood
will it be waking on these days,
pulling back the single curtain on the hot street,
on their own orchestrated dawn?
Or will it be strange landscapes from the air
that I have never seen?

One day there won't be this house,
this room, their three beds;
not even the faint rime
of salt on wings.

Lightning Catchers

Out of the hot September dark,
lightning and snakes in the grass,
the first few drops
pock the tractor tyres, the torn seat,
breaking the hold of heat
on the dusty fields.

Before a false dawn the thunder comes,
sheets of it
shaken out for folding over the hills.
Rabbits sitting upright by their dry bolt holes,
the parched slopes, their readiness for fire,
they all hear it: another song about how we live
in a tinderbox.

And look at us — out in the wild fields
with our bare feet and our lightning catchers,
jars for thunder, butterfly nets for rain.

You Don't Have to be Mary Oliver to Write a Poem about Geese

This is my church. I come here to worship
at the feet of redwoods and squirrels and monarch butterflies,
at the hem of the soft blue cloak of the sky.

I am sharing Nicasio Reservoir today
with a flock of Aleutian geese.
Now they have fed on the opposite shore,

too tall for their age, ungainly,
they slip into the water and glide serenely
across the lake. Beneath the surface

their webbed feet are working hard,
but in the world above water
their bodies slide along.

If I were Mary Oliver I might write a poem
about what a droll metaphor they are
for my poor, mud-speckled, stony-shored reservoir

of a life; about how they mirror
all my breathless paddling, the trying to keep up;
while here, in the world above water,

I glide towards the distant reeds,
all poise and ease and sleek feathers,
eyes forward, barely a ripple.

Bicycle Ride, Point Reyes

It isn't mine, the grey road
that wanders on down to the point
with its elk herds and cows
bellowing to be milked.

They don't belong to me, the snatches
of blue sea between the winded trees,
the painful greens, so like home,
the milk trucks lumbering by with their payload.

None of it is mine, but I borrow it
for a brief time, out gathering
the broken pieces of myself,
the loose hills reminding me

that today is about each rotation of my wheels,
only as important as the top of the next rise,
and when I die I shall be neither lost nor saved,
but borne up in the sweet arms of strangers.

Oak

When I came to you for love and comfort and shelter
I didn't even know I was coming to you
for love and comfort and shelter.

What could a gnarled and grizzled oak
holding its trembling arms above my cottage
know of love? Of comfort?

Each night in my narrow bed
I heard the twigs and the small acorns
knocking on my roof, the whispers,

and as I drifted far from shore,
hoping that sleep would keep me afloat,
I thought I heard you laughing quietly to yourself.

Mornings, outside my door,
those scratchy offerings, rimed, brown, curled —
I looked for messages there but none appeared.

I had never heard of oak heart, so stout and true,
hard as the winter freeze, cool as rain;
I had never heard you sing, until one day

I climbed to the top of your uneven stairs,
saw the world from the crown of your crown;
the fog touched my face, I let it; much later,

when the sky had rearranged her furniture
and I had searched in vain for the last stars
I climbed back down.

That was the morning of the first winter storm;
it blew so hard I was afraid to spread my wings,
but you cast your arms into the rain

as though there were no tomorrow, as though
you had it coming to you, all that noise and trouble,
and over it all you filled the wind with your singing.

The Island

We met — you were on your island,
quite alone among the palms and coconut shells,
the waves in your ears, the plaintive birds.
I favoured sunsets. I had a boat.
We sailed to the end of the sea but there wasn't much there
so we sailed back. The sun was long gone,
but the night was a queen, she invited us in;
her palace was silver and jewelled.
We lay on her velvet pillows, she poured us her dark,
and in the morning we feasted on coconuts and pearls.

Golden Temple

for Seamus

1

Show me your painted face
in the white and grey light of dawn,
imprint your soundless name
on the few simple things I own.
We may walk, arm in golden arm,
across the fractured canvas of this place
toward the perfect dome
while light from a primitive source
begins to write the surface of the Khan
and the colours of the hills,
but at this hour the gates are closed
against our fragile prayers.

2

I like this moment, and this,
and this. I have lowered my measuring stick
into the ancient water
where time divides in three and flows
coolly around our thighs. On the opposite bank,
rock without name; stories of old floods
whispered into stone. We may walk,
hand in hopeful hand,
across the forbidden bridge
like figures on a painted scroll
in the artist's hush of noon,
but each of us must know we walk alone.

3

Shadows collect in the crevices of rock.
There is a part of me that knows
we are each other's best work,
for we have walked, hearts of grace entwined,
to the temple, hungry for a sign
that this is not the only path through time,
and although we come away
without an answer carved in stone,
just look at how the river flows
without concern for our desires
and how the temple sends its rapturous spires
aloft, into the saffron-robed late afternoon.

Azimuth

1

It was June. It was a Friday.
I was walking in the orchard of our vows,
ripe pears, apples bending low.

I happened to be kneeling when you spoke:
'We are much farther north than we ever meant to be;
there is light in the sky at midnight here,

it comes around again just after four.
Do not fear, but I am going on alone
through towns redrawn since we were young.'

2

Afternoon, on a train. In the paper
news of a day you will never know
falls in ordered columns across my life.

On my hands river veins, maps of the years,
hands that anointed you with oils,
sandalwood, jojoba, lavender for rest.

But how to express — I need my mother tongue
for this — *l'étrangeté* — strangeness of the ghost
who walks alone inside my shoes.

3

Stripped January days, the marrow
holding on to winter, grief reinventing
its hold. Bleak as it may seem,

I ride the same train every afternoon,
laying holy miles between myself and home,
the angle of the sun due north along the horizon

lengthening. All I want is the miracle
of the morning newspaper
we shared; the pot of tea.

Glaces, Sorbets

Paris was grey this morning
out our tiny bathroom window.

One more book and we'll need new shelves;
the whole apartment knows it.

How many Fridays? Hundreds
and hundreds of Fridays, but never before

these particular leaves on the silk trees, such
a newborn green; this young sunshine, this wind.

I do not know how long we'll be married.
They say love hangs on for dear life,

hands at the throat,
until you cut it down.

Daisy Dress

My father drove, my brother sat in the back;
a picture hanging crooked from the start.
In the passenger seat, hushed world of white,
my hands did not belong, my thoughts weren't right.

Outside was everyone else's Saturday,
the parked cars, the vivid flowers.
We drove an unmarked Ford, no one could know,
to the tiny church that would swallow me whole.

My mother travelled in an earlier car,
twisting in her lap the long and the short:
not the son of the framer, not our village church,
nor the feast of neighbours gathering eager on the porch

for a glimpse of the bride. In sudden memory
I stood on the grass in my daisy dress at nine,
my grandmother smiling vaguely off to port,
my mother, black hair worn fashionably short,

hugging even then her secrets to herself;
familiar as the stars, unknowable,
unreachable, though I kissed her every night,
smiling and fluttering against the bars in fright.

Nineteen years later on this endless coastal drive
in our unmarked car — *was that a bride?* —
the wind took my childhood, whipped it like a kite,
up, over the treeless land, and on, out of sight.

The 49-mile Scenic Drive

Miles one to five, dangerously married,
it was good to be on this earth, together,
and alive.

Around mile six everything changed
as everything has so many times.
He began to cheat

on me every night with a bottle
and an ashtray. The things we
carry around.

I looked in the storefront windows
as we passed, I looked in the doorways;
people were living there.

Pain is relative. Mile seventeen
I unhooked the bracelet of lies.
Suffering

may be a higher form of truth,
and he did swear he would stop;
but I knew.

I got out of the car. I handed
him his half of all of it back.
It was raining,

that blurry San Francisco sort of mist
that mingles with the blood
and tears.

Fairfax Theater

for Mallory

From where they are they can see the town,
all the houses and the way people live,
the blazons of cities and the far stars,
the moon on the waves like jewellery.

But one looks only to casting signs
in the stark light. He likes the work,
stringing promises above the town,
loves the creaking hush when the lights go down
and the music wears its white dress down the aisle.
Cigarette girls with their trays and their nylon desires
make him smile, third row from the back,
holding his wife's warm hand in her ample lap.

The other looks out on the town.
He's watching his picture as it's happening
with its scenes of flying and drowning;
he'd like to stay till dawn
when the night sky blows back out to sea
and burnoff reveals the hungry light,
lean on the hills. He knows his life
is a shout in the dark: those childhood summers
that went out like tall ships, the matches struck
for birthday candles, his desperate rowing
so as not to seem adrift upon the waters of his luck.

Behind them now —
the family man and the castaway —
the marquee breaks its movie news of the hour,
a simple plan for a fleeting week in time,
and all across town
the first bells of night are being rung,
long and silver-tongued and blue mooned.

Warm Bodies, Cold Bodies

It is not yet the end of the day,
it is not quite winter. He has left
the house of books and telescopes,
bird guides and field glasses, warm hearth,
and the two who live without hope,
for the cold and delicate aria of the deep.

This is the dead son
of the lovely couple up in the old house,
theirs the vacant deckchairs;
his motionless form, cold to their warm,
watches the vast and restless coming and going,
no two waves the same.

Birds sweep wide in their loose flocks;
a hundred yards offshore,
in the lazy pull beyond the breakers' cream,
the humpback rolls in the gloom
still needing to rise for air,
whalebone straining the plates for krill.

Up at the house
they long for their son, but he doesn't feel.
He does not feel. Their pain,
old as history, big as a whale,
shifts uneasily in the home
they filled with treasures for their only one.

A hundred miles away
the humpback's moan — a half-hour,
complex, mourning song —
is caught by other whales and carried on
across the endless concert hall
of the ocean floor.

In his kick-down deckchair
he feels the tidal pull, and it makes sense
to let his moorings loose,
he who used to have prayers,
someone to say them to,
a way of kneeling before the bed.

Where He Is Now

He was told it would be like flying,
like winged horses: take-off, then the rise
over the fog-bound cities, above the black winds
that tear at the earth's waist, and on
to where sun breaks on the stones,
and the women wear bright cloth,
carry water.

He thought death would be all altitude.
Instead, this languorous drown:
breathing the shallows, with every inhalation
more saurian, more tug-of-the-moon;
he lays his cold cheek against the river's hunger,
the dark, umbilical shadow he rides,
still warm, long as his own frame,
and listens deep in its watery flumes
where the old sounds rise like vapours.

'Slow,' says his life,
'I am no vessel for your griefs —
those elusive loves,
the careless rooms of childhood's hiding,
father's boots on the bare boards,
blunt afternoons, the heavy bus to school —

for we move together toward the falls,
the Lethean pools where all men turn in the end,
and if I am a glass
in which you glimpse your sorrowful face
think of me also as that girl in her cambric dress
you once crushed in your wild embrace.

Lie still
and let the river take us.'

The Angel of Poetry

The honeymakers of the world are lying low,
but that doesn't mean they do not feel their wings,
only that when the light is finally gone
and almost all words are missing or cannot be said
they will rise up lightly from their beds,
hearts like fists, rivers flowing fast
beneath their ice, and illuminate the night.

The artists of the world are tired;
they have emptied out till they are just containers;
this is how their music, painting, words, and songs
come flooding in. For now, all they share
are snatches of the same dark fire, all they know
is that they wear their lives as loosely
as the wind making patterns on the snow.

There are bees at the flowers in December. It is not right
to live like this down here in the half-light.
The angel of poetry might be the last who remembers
why we did this to ourselves: it is he
who with his cold white wings makes the ice sing,
makes the chainsaws sob like hungry children,
and the birds rise in consternation over the robbed earth.

And have no doubt: it will also be he who comes
at your final hour, making the curtain billow at your door.
He will take your burning heart in both his hands;
he will shake out your desires and whisper in your ear:
Don't you know me? I am part of the pattern
that time makes lovely and destroys.
Now it's your turn to fly — don't you feel your wings?

Jar and Flower

I was out choosing willows for stakes
when you wrote your note.

The young girl you thought you knew from her letters
had never shown.

I thought we had our own language, like twins,
a pair of charcoal birds

loosely drawn up in the eaves of our home
among the soft moths,

soaking up the sense of rain and the simple intervals
that might sustain us;

but the fall showers were bringing down the brick dust
and grime of our tenure

and the fall wind in the trees had last year's clothes shaken
    loose
like small change.

I had to scramble lest I go under in the sudden tumble of
    water
beneath our bridges.

Every dawn the city turned inside out and every night
was broken

by the black fan turning, turning endlessly in the gloom.
I should have known.

I should have been bold, ridden off on the wildest of my
    dreams,
but I lingered

in our hollow room, with the stigma of rain on glass, the
    cracked jar,
and the single flower.

All Souls Passing Over

Today of all days you can almost see through the veil;
due respect to the white bones and the hags
with snakes for hair, one glance at their awful beauty

inviting remorse; the trees in the river's mirror
are almost there, almost on the other side,
their hesitating makes the water shiver

and though you may tell yourself in all earnestness
those are just the forked limbs of willows
reflected in a surface, you also know

that faint splashing to be the oars of some
ferryman who rises out of the mist
with the look of a clock maker you once knew

and takes from his pocket something meaningful,
like a key that unlocks the gate you have been
gazing at the garden through since you were little.

Aquifer

On my rooftop, with its view of the casbah
and the sea, I am hanging clothes to dry;
I work because my solace is in work.

These are the facts: the sea and the minarets,
and the flowered cloth I was once about to burn
because I was wearing it the day I heard.

What is the name of my house?
Alone on the street in the relentless desert air
its walls saturate. My house is an aquifer;

even the red winds cannot dry it out.
Beneath the angry tiles, behind cool stone,
the call to sorrow comes at dawn, at noon,

but toward evening as the water table rises
those furies who range around my home
looking to punish all who shed blood, make strife

retire to their still forms in the clay;
my fingers brush against them in the airless night.
If I had not worn that dress,

if the sun were held back from its careless ascent
and if you had not been lost,
I would still be singing you this ghostly little song.

The Influence of Ghosts

Call me no phantom, nor ghoul,
certainly no angel.
I walk about like anybody else,
silent words of solace to the passersby,
a nod to the patrons at the street café
where the others still sit and have tea.

I loved my life with a fierce joy.
At the summit I was twenty-six
thousand feet up, the air was pure.
I was breathing heaven, soaring
you could call it, master of my
patchwork world down there.

Then came descent, the inevitable
memory lapses, lines, a heavier body.
I began to read the hidden writing:
one day I would have to step outside
my frame of reference, dim the lighting,
walk away without a backward glance.

It was a time of deprivation,
hunger, the trees doing without their leaves.
I went down on my knees; it seemed
the place to be. My cells
cried out in unison, *abandon us! abandon us!*
The world had never bled so much

nor looked so radiant, so profuse,
nor sweet, nor comforting to me.
The wind rolled through the cottonwoods
like labour pains; I had to wail aloud.
It was the end of the end,
there was no limit to my sorrow.

Brush all thought from your heart,
it was not made for waiting.
At this chance moment of our meeting
do you not look through me as you pause,
arrested by a sudden fleeting sense
that you are held and clearly seen

and known? For my part I will not falter.
I am one step from reading
what is in your palm. I am
the gentle voice you're almost hearing.
Are you listening? The secret is,
at last, that losing everything

makes perfect sense. It cannot be
another way. Far out to sea
the ships ride low on the horizon
burdened with their cargo of men's dreams,
while here on shore sleep comes down
despite longing, easy and unknowing.

The Nearest Exit

We are waiting at the station for our train to arrive.
Our shadows crouch like insects and although
the screens tell us all trains will be on time
it's hard to be alive.

The heart has been a dangerous place for us.
That's why we sit without looking up,
escape routes inked on our palms, trying to evolve
without goals or intention or design.

If you were one like us with the nameless reflection
and the slender past, you too might
cast your eyes about for the nearest exit;
you too might learn to run as fast

as the fastest boy. Bone, teeth, shells,
we are all put together the same way,
and though we die we surely lie down
further than death each night.

Lately we all seem to have lost the same
pearly thing we cannot name,
and we have come to blame love as the fire
we have all been throwing each other.

Not all that gutters can be rekindled
to its old pale flame. If I were the driver
of that train I would take us all home,
into the darkest moment of the storm.

Elegy for Kate

Some people's lives make a smooth arc,
some are stepped, some jagged,
snapped at a junction like a brittle stick,
like the greedy day
fate took her white coat
and hung it on a nail in an empty house;
her life narrowed from a generous past
and began to gather dust; the flowers starved,
the streams ran dry. On the other side of night
the trains mourned by; she could hear them
from inside her roomful of rearranged things
where she struggled to make out the words
by the dark light of a single bulb.

Yesterday the heavy cloak of the future,
the unnameable troubles of the past,
were taken from her shoulders, hung on the wind,
and she walked unencumbered at last.
A cloud of angels lay across the half-moon
as she closed the book of her life, though a little light
still shines out from between the pages.

Untwinned

When we were hanging
we always hung together.
That was the code,
the secret handshake
of our amniotic fellowship.
You broke it
when you hung alone,
and I had to take that
SwissTool Spirit Plus
Dad gave you
in a moment of innocence
and cut you down.

It didn't help
that everyone was so sorry.
Some say
the dead are always near.
You weren't at the funeral.
You weren't even
in the hemisphere.
Why would you hover
at the scene
of such extraordinary pain —
especially once
you knew where you were going?

The creek light
is playing on the underside
of the bay and gold locust
and chestnut leaves.
The creek is running away.
Never mind about
the Frank-Starling law of the heart
(the chambers will pump out
as much as they get);

some loads
are too much
for the strongest ventricles;

some packs too heavy
for even the bravest girls.

Meals for Friends

My friend Clara couldn't hold a book any more:
too heavy. She was near her time and she knew it.
The birds around the house all sang to it,
a sweet adagio in the cottonwoods,
discreet white curtain blowing in the breeze,
flickering sun through the spring leaves.

Vern could hardly get to the door in the end,
blinds all drawn, TV on high so he could hear,
apricots falling into nets from the tree by the gate.
The yellowjackets feasted on them.
Then Vern's body gave out. He died.
His son got dinners for a while.

Everything I needed to remember
has been remembered; everything I yearned to forget
is lost. Who knows what future, who cares what past,
the night sky is no longer far away,
the ocean gives its undivided attention
to the fall of the Dog Star, the moon's invitation.

I feel I've been here a long time,
climbing these ladders, climbing these stairs.
I wish I had built more fences, taken down more fences,
but other than that my prayers
largely went unanswered and what matter now
when the heart has proved such a porous vessel for love?

59th Street Bridge

The city through the bridge's fenestrated limbs
hums its own tuneless songs.
This is where I come when I need to live alone,
to pay back all the borrowed time.
I know what you are murmuring:
you cannot hide, you cannot run.
But I have this to say: the time for flight has come.
Give me a small craft on the river,
give me a raft I can set sail on;
there will be no end to my tether.
I will pull myself along by Orion's belt,
I will power my strokes with the four gas giants,
and when the first waves come
I will do as all children of the sea are born to do:
stay out there until dinner is no longer being served
and the only ones left on the beach
are an old man and his faithful hound.
And should I run aground on a sandy shoal
I will break my fast on the stars, drink the darkness
down to its bitter grounds.
There are gaps in a life big enough to clamber through,
chinks in the girders you can see the future
and the sky through, and the end of the sky
where it falls below its busy line;
and the buildings and the bridges and the traffic
turn on their axes and turn again.
And now it is time. I am taking off my shoes.

Shelter

for Alfie

Back at the old house after so long
I stand in the kitchen doorway:
this was where they carried him down the long hall,
the bedroom where he lay, so many times too small
for his own suit; that was him
deep in the ancient woods of his final day,
but that was not him they lowered
into the bitter, unforgiving clay.

The last time I spoke with him
we were cracking jokes about the pain,
sunning on the beach of our imagining,
crystal water, sand like silk.
Will I ever laugh like that again?
Ever ride high on the pleasure
of my going on alone?
Or will I stay Alice: some days too tall,
some too small, lost in Wonderland,
never able for the low door in the wall
when the key is in my hand.

This was the way they passed with him.
It could have been a stretcher, maybe a bier;
it was his lightness broke us all,
but he asked to be let go: he was ready, he said.
It must have been the brush of a wingtip at his ear;
and one day I too will be loosed,
released to the wind, and the wind will shelter me
briefly in her arms before I'm free.

Ghost, Soho

When I fall to earth,
to the crowded streets,
among the people and their smouldering histories,
it's the sharpness of the light that helps me
move about, but it's their hunger drives me.

Make no mistake: I am alone in my film,
a man with no lines to speak of,
a ghost among the girls with their restless searching;
I turn the world down low
until I begin to hear their silent lives.

Beneath the doorway conversations
they're trying on their futures in the glare of the afternoon,
and in the space between their longing and their pride,
faced with the death of time,
they're praying, though I can't make out the words.

Nights I lie beneath the friendless stars,
their thoughts the same
as when Persephone ate her seven seeds,
but down here in the homes of men
they're naming their daughters after sorrow.

Within the pitiless walls they begin
to know what they have lost.
I watch their grief
rise in wreaths against the roof of the world
and the centuries go by, too fast, too slow.

Park Bench, Queens

Haven't been this far away before
from the centre, never been this slight.
Takes years to piece together
such a broken life. Have I been called?
They said I would be called.

Just sitting here is taking all my strength.
Such a dark part of the puzzle
being half awake, much turned to bitter dust,
cold coffee in a paper cup between my hands,
the past nailed up in a bone box.

I go under, I come back up for air;
the wrecking ball is still there, poised
above my life in black and white;
the dirt spirals up in human forms,
cars crawl by on all fours.

The wheels turn, the wheels turn,
we see much more than we can later recall;
some distance from the fork in the road
I turn and look the way I have come,
step by step away from my last home.

It hasn't always been like this,
and even if I cannot see
the sunlight draining down the mountains
or the bats swirling out of their cave
in a half wheel, there is a limit to my trouble.

I do count the flurries of winter birds
drawn in crayon against a wayward sky.
Half my picture may have come away
from the other half, the colours wrung out,
but when the ground shakes I have my bench,

my own place, the sun that someone sprayed
on the overpass, and the ordinary voices
layering human story over the rain.
Some days only children see me
without fear, without grief.

How It Will End

There are
days like this on earth:
upper windows fling their arms wide open
on the Persian blue,
caged birds beat their wings
and the heart escapes its bars.

Days like this, the rain
still weeks away, the parched earth
letting loose its finer dust with every breath,
life is a ceremony, simple among the redwoods,
each of us in our own shaft of celestial light
bearing down like truth.

But sometimes the past comes forward,
lit from behind, voices off.
It's dark. Half a moon, stars.
The bow across the strings calls forth
a new low tone we have never heard;
the walls of happiness, already paper thin,
threaten to come down. Sadness opens up
like an umbrella, blotting out
the night, and the moon's frail voice
whispers secrets that we cannot properly discern:
this, she is saying, is how time began,

and this —
in the unearthly hush of 3 a.m.
with the gentle back and forth
between two walnut trees
of owls in their parliament —
this is how it will end.

Barstools, North Beach

Of all the rooms in which I've asked to be set free
this is the emptiest. I am not sure
who I was looking for.

Eventually I will have eaten
all the food in my house.
There will be no more food.

When that day comes, what use love?
The scudding pink clouds may be pregnant with it
but I'll have no call for it.

I will be feasting on bones.
I will be waiting here with the barstools
and the last slant of the sun,

the future a foreign country
where I do not speak the language
and there is nobody I know.

I dreamed my other children,
but they did not come.
In the dream I painted rooms for them;

I named them all, held them
in a radiant storm of light and sound, and then
I left them there: waiting to be found.

If every day is holy, full of miracles,
why does the sun go down?
Why do the windows open on oblivion?

∾

Yet if the future really is a foreign place
I like to think of it as endless meadows,
brown streams,

and when it is done
they can scatter me among the Mexican Gold,
the fire poppies and columbines,

and who knows:
tomorrow I may still be alive,
still dancing.

Absolution

Woke up to the year's midnight,
no more moon, no stars,
little black birds with the crimson hearts
strung out on the wires at the day's start,
frail pair-oar pushed out on the reservoir.
I thought the world was turning,
now I'm not sure.

The last day of the year:
there is currently nowhere to hide
the poverty or desire,
want, scarcity, need; there aren't even
adequate words for it
down here in the wreckage;
may we all somehow be pulled free.

I'm at the low-water mark
and I want the journey back.
I sold it, or someone stole it,
and now those same little birds
with the bleeding throats
can hardly sing their way past
the dark stain of hunger, the loneliness

of not sitting down to eat every day,
the drought of tomorrow's empty bowl.
On the surface of the water
rain falls as it pleases, in waves.
Come spring, after the long months
of slumbering, I want my life
to unfurl again, transcendent green;

I want to come to the end
of coming to the end, begin again
as though there had never been

that sparse, underfed exhaustion,
as though the cup were always brimful,
the world turning constantly from depletion
toward forgiveness, absolution.

Rain at Easter

It's never rained like this before
at Easter. Where the colours should be pale yellow,
pale blue, they are an unremitting slate.
Nobody's out catching fish in Kent Lake.
The storm blew every leaf off the rain tree
in the paddock; it's standing naked against the sky
freed of its burden, no more falling;
and although the willows are tired of weeping
our hearts beat on, unconcerned with beating,
spring rolls around regardless of who's waiting,
the raptors swing steeply on the wing
and the heavy drops beat the tulips down
into their final embrace with life.
The silence is continually broken,
but it's still there beneath the rushing water
in all its pieces.

This I Take With Me

This I take with me:
whales spouting, wind blowing the cares off,
the bells of the town crying *Come down! come down!*
April in with a wild flurry of rain,
I bow down before her,
I give her all praise and blame.

This I leave behind:
lies so deep you could rest your life on them,
love turning with the leaves,
age — it doesn't mean too much,
sticks in the sand, stone markers
at regular intervals along the strand.

It's quiet out here:
mist over many hills, the odd car,
spillway in full spill.
I seem to have missed the order
to march forth, but march forth I will
into the silent blue future nobody can hear.

Boathouse

Everybody has an old deserted boathouse they drive down to
in their secondhand car, swimming naked from the jetty,
sometimes going under, the thin green weed for hair,
but always coming up for lungfuls of the grey-white air.

Along the narrow lane to my boathouse
the trees stand up, as at a funeral, in their new clothes;
in the ditches shooting stars and forget-me-nots I never planted
arise, fragile and lovely, without my care.

Because I cannot sleep in a cave in a heavy bed
with the relentless move to entropy that the second law entails
and the yaw and roll of our too-small planet
pitching among the meteors and the flashing dust clouds;

because of the three stars in a row outside my skylight —
just staying there, no comfort in stars any more —
and the slavering of the wolf outside my door,
I have driven down to this last refuge of lovers and thieves.

Whatever has me staring fixedly into the darkness
maybe I can haul it out of the trunk, bury it in the shaley sand,
maybe I just want my thoughts to stand by themselves
by the edge of the gentle water so I do not have to drive
    them around

anymore, to be eaten alive by their hunger.
Eventually I will be here more than anywhere else,
wading out every night, every morning waking out of the too-
    cold water
to the stillness that is just what it is. This. Here. Now.

Acknowledgements

Acknowledgments are due to the editors and publishers of the following, in which some of these poems have previously appeared: *An Anthology of Modern Irish Poetry* (Harvard University Press), *Marin Poetry Anthology, The Pedestal Magazine, Poetry Ireland Review* and *When the Muse Calls* (Pomegranate Press).